WORK IN REGRESS

Also by Peter Reading

Collected Poems:
1: Poems 1970-1984
(Bloodaxe Books, 1995)

Water and Waste (1970)
For the Municipality's Elderly (1974)
The Prison Cell & Barrel Mystery (1976)
Nothing For Anyone (1977)
Fiction (1979)
Tom o' Bedlam's Beauties (1981)
Diplopic (1983)
5x5x5x5x5 (1983)
C (1984)

Collected Poems:
2: Poems 1985-1996
(Bloodaxe Books, 1996)

Ukulele Music (1985)
Going On (1985)
Stet (1986)
Final Demands (1988)
Perduta Gente (1989)
Shitheads (1989)
Evagatory (1992)
Last Poems (1994)
Eschatological (1996)

Chinoiserie (The Bay Press, 1997)
[limited edition: 20 Charlie Street,
Greenside, Ryton NE40 4AQ]

WORK IN REGRESS

Peter Reading

BLOODAXE BOOKS

ISBN: 1 85224 421 6

First published 1997 by
Bloodaxe Books Ltd,
P.O. Box 1SN,
Newcastle upon Tyne NE99 1SN.

Bloodaxe Books Ltd acknowledges
the financial assistance of Northern Arts.

Cover printing by J. Thomson Colour Printers Ltd, Glasgow.

Printed in Great Britain by
Cromwell Press Ltd, Broughton Gifford, Melksham, Wiltshire.

To the poet's parents

Acknowledgements

'Gula' was commissioned by the South Bank Centre as part of its Poetry International 1996 Festival.

'Three' was commissioned by BBC Radio 3 to celebrate fifty years of its existence.

Contents

11 Three
17 Fireworks
18 Shropshire Lads
19 The farewell
20 Mimnermian
21 Seed
22 Shakespearean
23 Nomenclature
24 Ovidian
27 Horatian
28 Integration
29 Nips
30 'Prince Urges the West to Learn from Islam'
31 Propertian
32 *I.M.*, G.MacB.
33 From the Chinese
34 Gula
36 *I.M.*, G. E.
37 Callimachan
38 *Raphus cucullatus*
40 *En Attendant*
41 Theognian
42 Nips
43 [Untitled]
44 From the Chinese
45 Catullan
46 'Clear Beggars from Streets, says Blair'
47 From the Chinese
48 Salopian
49 Obit
50 [Untitled]
51 Tristia
52 Theocritan
54 [Untitled]
55 OED
56 Luger
57 [Untitled]
58 Propertian
61 Distich

(Desperate Circumstances
demand disparate measures.)

Three

1946:
the first post-war bananas
arrive in Britain; Churchill
receives the Order of Merit;
three-year-old treated to four
bananas dies of the overdose;
Government plans to spend
380 million
on building 'New Towns' to 'encourage
a sense of culture and pride
in those who will live in them';
the Jitterbug hits Brit ballrooms;
John Logie Baird dies;
H.G. Wells dies;
Granville Bantock dies;
Hermann Goering dies;
W.C. Fields dies;
Ladislao Biro invents
the ball-point pen; the Beeb
engenders the Third Programme;
Peter Reading is born.

                    *

'70: 4,000 Brits
die of Asian flu
in week ending January 2nd;
Bertrand Russell dies
aged 97; Nixon
sends US troops to Cambodia;
E.M. Forster dies;
the great Mark Rothko dies;
Heath is elected PM;
Tynan concocts *Oh! Calcutta!*
Palestinian hijackers
blow up some Boeings (of course);
Mary Wilson (Harold's
missus) publishes poems
(price 12 shillings, nice);

missiles are hurled at the stage
during the Miss World contest;
Pravda slams Solzhenitsyn...

Also, George MacBeth
is presenting *Poetry Now*
on the wireless's Third Programme
and invites Peter Reading
to Broadcasting House to record
his own valedictory poem
in his own ugly voice
(half-a-lifetime younger):
Evenings are drawing in quickly,
we sip dry Sherry, it darkens,
decanters of Sauternes for plasma,
the central heating is love-fired
against the chill of the evenings,
evenings are drawing in quickly...
In the BBC Club an hour later,
sipping a Fino or two,
George recalls early days
and working with Louis MacNeice,
remarks how, though he once shared
an office with him , he never
felt that he knew the loner.
Then, naturally, the chat
turns to grim Demise.
MacBeth posits his theory
that friends who happen to die
are merely the same as those
whom we know to exist but don't see.
Well, *maybe*, Reading opines,
and commits the hypothesis
to oblivion, till, years later,
his best mate is flensed in a car crash
and his own ugly voice
records in a monotone:
You used Propertius once
to Preface a ghost poem – Sunt
aliquid manes, letum
non omnia finit...

And now George MacBeth himself
(who, somehow, seemed unassailable
by mortal distemper) is dead,
and Reading remembers the Langham,
the talk and the subsequent tapes,
and hears his own ugly voice
(half-a-life younger) and George
mispronouncing 'Reading',
and regrets that he failed on that
and other occasions to say
'Thank you, George, and goodbye'.

*

1971:
Sonny Liston dies;
Idi Amin stages coup;
the great Stravinsky dies;
Arsenal wins the Cup;
Ogden Nash dies;
Louis Armstrong dies;
riots flare in Ulster;
first Baron Reith dies;
Northern Ireland – another
1,500 troops
are sent to the bloody province;
BBC swamped with complaints
when a boy uses four-letter-word
on, of all things, *Woman's Hour*;
Nikita Khrushchev dies;
the hits of '71 –
'My Sweet Lord', 'Maggie May',
and 'Chirpy, Chirpy, Cheep, Cheep'...

And I listen again to the voices –
George MacBeth mispronouncing
'Reading' and Reading reading
half-a-life younger, stridulous:
All must return to our dusty
origins sometime, all
must return to our dusty origins...

*

1980: Sir Cecil
Beaton pops his clogs;
Graham Sutherland dies;
Oskar Kokoschka dies;
Hitchcock and Tito die;
Iranian Embassy stormed;
Henbit wins the Derby;
Henry Miller dies;
Peter Sellers dies;
Iraq attacks Iran;
Iran attacks Iraq;
Jeremy Isaacs chosen
to head fourth TV channel;
fuck knows who shot JR;
Oswald Mosley, friend
of Mussolini and Hitler,
dies (somewhat belatedly)…

and the voice of George MacBeth
from sixteen years ago
announces 'Alma Mater',
to be followed by nasal growlings…

Sunt aliquid manes.

*

1982:
civil unrest in Bristol;
Thelonious Monk dies;
Carl Orff and 'Rab' Butler die;
Argentina invades the Falklands;
Israel invades Lebanon;
Henry Fonda dies;
Ingrid Bergman dies;
Group Captain Bader dies;
Glenn Gould dies;
Jacques Tati dies;
Arthur Askey dies;
'Bad Language' on Channel 4!;
man gets mechanical heart;
the women at Greenham Common
are carted away by Old Bill;

Reading is reading 'Dark Continent'
and 'The Terrestrial Globe'...

*

1984:
Johnny Weissmuller dies;
the halfpenny piece is phased out;
acid rain threatens UK;
Torvill and Dean win a gold
at the Sarajevo Olympics;
William 'Count' Basie dies;
Tito Gobbi dies;
Sir John Betjeman dies;
Eric Morecambe dies;
at last!, the 'Greenhouse Effect';
the level of childhood leukaemia
is ten times the national average
around Sellafield nuclear plant;
James F. Fixx (the man
who turned America on
to jogging) dies (while jogging)
of a massive heart attack;
J.B. Priestley dies;
Truman Capote dies;
Richard Burton dies;
Islamic suicide bomber
kills 40 in US Embassy
in mad bloody East Beirut;
Indira Gandhi shot dead;
famine in Ethiopia;
Reagan romps to victory.

The hits of '84:
'I just called to say I love you',
'Do they know it's Christmas?', 'Relax'.

On BBC Radio 3,
Reading is reading a poem
concerning the hapless fishermen
caught in the blast and fall
of the Bikini explosion
(Sunt aliquid manes)...

*

1996:
Reading recording this,
thinks of George MacBeth's proposition
that friends who happen to die
are merely the same as those
whom we know to exist but don't see,
Sunt aliquid manes,
letum non omnia finit,
and is assailed by the voices,
Sunt aliquid manes,
letum non omnia finit,
and the rewinds, stops, fast-forwards,
and thinks of how Gavin Ewart
(avuncular, unassuming,
genial eroticist,
laureate of levity,
champ of the flyweight poem,
angry, compassionate, sensitive,
at once amused and appalled)
would have been 80 this year...

and thinks how the carnage continues,
and of how he will soon be part of it,
Sunt aliquid manes,

Sunt aliquid manes,

Sunt aliquid manes,

Sunt aliquid manes,

Sunt aliquid manes,

Sunt aliquid manes,

Sunt aliquid manes,

Sunt aliquid manes,

Sunt aliquid manes...

Fireworks

The shelling is heavy tonight;
if we survive till tomorrow
there'll be nettle soup and black bread.

Shropshire Lads

Thick mist enswathes the Prison at Shrewsbury;
a bloke I know inside would dearly wish
to be on this train bound for benign Ludlow.

*

Places of interest in this town include:
Ludlow Museum, Ludlow Castle... [and
the Hen & Chickens, where, each Friday night,
the Smiths and Bradleys thump each other shitless].

The farewell,

the fumbled embrace,
the suddenly otiose kiss,
the Tannoy *regrets that this...*
twenty-eight years late,
the solo stroll to the end
of the platform wherefrom the sleepers
recede and recede and recede.

Mimnermian [Mimnermus (*fl.* 630 BC)]

Just as new petals sparkling in springtime
   quicken in sunlight,
      so do we burgeon in youth
      reckless of impartial Zeus.

Two Fates attend us: one is the bane, the
   fruit of our dotage;
      one is the blessing of death
      ending our nonage's bloom.

When the brief blossom is done, to die is
   better than living
      haplessly plagued by the dread
      of penury, grief and the grave.

Painful longevity, chance death early,
   death of one's children –
      infinite is the ill-luck
      on the Olympian list.

Seed

Onto the pile of the Axminster fluffs of
    willowherb settle.
        Autumn: the wanton swing-doors
        splay to admit this spent seed.

Shakespearean

Someone I know was lolling in the doorway
of a stuffy factory office where he worked
absorbing early April UV rays
when down the yard the General Manager
came striding clad in a protective white
crisp overall against industrial grime.
The gaffer twitched an eyebrow then observed:
'I see you *like* the sun; a nice bright day?'
The idler laconically riposted:
'It is the bright day that brings forth the adder;
and that craves wary walking.' One week later
Head Office sent him his P45.

Nomenclature

The marriage vows:
Lead Albatross.

The only child:
A Second Chance.

The railway fare:
Pence on the Tongue.

The air-hostess:
Grim Charonis.

The civic bronze:
Persephone.

Ovidian

Banished, maybe, but the fame of Naso
  possibly lives on
    still in the City where men
    mention my name with respect.

Those who still spare me a thought should know the
  fate I endure here
    on this forgotten stark shore
    under the frost-sharpened stars.

I am surrounded by hordes of barbarians –
  which tribe is foulest
    I am unable to judge
    for they seem equally vile.

In the short summer the river protects us
  from an invasion
    but, when it freezes, the hordes
    cross the thick ice to maraud.

Snow falling constantly whipped by the wind lies
  heavy and hardens,
    sun will not thaw it, nor rain,
    more falls and settles on top.

Here the indigenous swaddle themselves in
  pelts of the wild beasts –
    all one can see is their beards
    riddled with sparkling rime.

Wine freezes hard, the bottle-shaped lumps they
  cleave with machetes,
    serving it solid to suck,
    crunch on or melt in the mouth.

Water is chiselled like stone from the lakes; the
  Danube is hard-paved;
    where the boats bobbed, horses pound,
    trundling oxen-carts cross;

even the sea ices over – I've often
   walked on its surface
      slithering on the tough shell
      safe from the water beneath

(now, had the Hellespont been so composed, the
   hapless Leander
      could have walked calmly across
      wisely eschewing the waves);

dolphins, unable to arch from the brine, are
   trapped by the ice crust;
      breakers, solidified, grasp
      shipping and fish in a vice.

Over the ice-bridge as soon as it forms the
   barbarous horsemen
      gallop with thunderous strength,
      whipping their steeds into froth,

pillaging, savagely sacking the farmsteads,
   taking the women.
      Villagers, terrified, hide,
      flee from the venom-barbed shafts.

Then the marauders swoop on the prize of
   untended livestock,
      implements, carts and such things,
      leaving the hovels in flames.

Those who are taken and tied up turn to
   see their homes blazing;
      that which the raiders don't want
      they systematically wreck.

After the raid the survivors remain in
   great trepidation,
      loth to return to the plough,
      dreading another attack,

so that the fields lie abandoned and always
   barren and blighted –
      no vineyards, no foamy vats,
      no orchards bearing rich fruit.

This is a land where, unless a man is
   dogged by misfortune,
      he should not venture to be;
      my lot it is to live here.

Horatian

Nunc est bibendum
(then address the issue of
  cheesy pudendum).

Integration

Between the Bookie and the Balti House
a grim homunculus purveys the *Echo*,
but periodically he sallies forth
to cow his patrons with a raised clenched fist,
and they are clearly discomposed by this.

The, ahem, Hospital *discharged him early —
they have a serious shortage of resources...*

He's been ensconced here for about two years
and we take something from him every day,
and by this regular sociability
it's hoped we all shall soon be integrated.

Nips

'No,' I replied when
my Aunt Prudence said to me
   'Give up the drink,' '*No.*'

*

Chaos rife outside;
I fuss about in the house
   tidying things up.

*

Ill-concealed contempt
is, perhaps, what I evinced
   when the rep. walked in.

*

Everybody knows
someone devoid of talent –
   I know more than most.

'Prince Urges the West to Learn from Islam'

(*The Times* headline 14. XII. 96)

Islam (that loudmouth jackass the Prince of
  Wales has advised us)
offers alternative values to wicked
  Westernist Science.
How many times does one have to reiterate
  worldly Lucretius?:
Tantum religio potuit sua-
  dere malorum.

Propertian (III. viii)

What a wonderful row
   last night by candlelight!
What fine abuse spat
   from your lunatic lips
when, violent with wine,
   you kicked over the table
and viciously hurled
   your glass at my head!

Come on! Attack me!
   Rip out my hair!
Scar my face
   with your elegant nails!
Threaten to scorch
   my eyeballs out
with a brand from the fire!
   Wrench my shirt open,
tear it to tatters!

   There is no true love
without altercation –
   let *un*quarrelsome girls
be reserved alone
   for those I despise.

Let everyone look at
   my neck's raw love-bites;
let my contusions
   show I have been with you;
lend our love anguish –
   my tears or yours;
glower your admonishment;
   gesture obscenely.

I have no use
   for untroubled sleep.
Rage at me always
   while I wilt with pallor.

The last thing I want
   from *you* is a quiet life!

I.M., **G.MacB.**

Twenty-six years ago, sipping a Fino or
  two in the Langham,
    You and I spoke of the grave,
    also of Li Po *et al.*

How the departure of friends on a lengthy
  journey was somewhat
    similar to their demise –
    suddenly, they were not *here.*

How the convention of giving a willow wand
  to a departing
    friend who is travelling far
    features in much of Du Mu.

I said I thought it absurd to talk to the
  dead in a poem –
    death, *ipso facto*, precludes
    cosy perusal of verse.

    'Just a convention, of course,
    just a convention,' you said.

From the Chinese

Frost crisp in moonlight,
the delicate catkin trembles.

I bend a sprig and it snaps –
too late to present it to you!

Gula

'The scene here described with such vivid dramatic power took place, it is evident, in some large ale-house in London, not very far from Cock Lane, Smithfield, from Cheapside, and from Garlickhithe. It was also probably very near a church. It is a very curious fact, that there is absolutely no reason why the Boar's Head, in Eastcheap, immortalised by Shakespeare, should not have been the very tavern here meant...it boasted to be the "chief tavern in London", and (which is very curious) its back windows looked out on to the burial ground of St Michael's, a church which is now pulled down, but has given its nane to St Michael's Lane.'

W.W. SKEAT, notes to *PIERS THE PLOWMAN*

Glutton was going . to get himself shriven,
and made for St Michael's . to confess his misdemeanours.
But Beton, of the Boar's Head, . bawled out 'Good morning!',
asked where was he walking to?, . what was he going for?
'To St Michael's,' he answered, . 'I mean to hear Mass –
I'll be shrived and shown . the shame of my sins.'
'But my beer is the best – . take a bench, drink a bellyful.'
Then Glutton goes in, . and a great gang after him:
Cicely (the shoemaker) . sat on the settle;
Watt (who keeps cattle) . called in with his wife;
Tim (the tinker) . and two of his trainees;
Hick (who hires horses) . and Hugh (who sells needles);
Clarice, of *Cock* Lane, . courting the clerk;
there were pickpockets; whores; . the hangman of Tyburn;
David (the ditch-digger) . with a dozen degenerates;
Sir Piers of Predie; . Pernell from Flanders;
a rebec fiddler; . a rogue; a felon;
a ratcatcher chap; . a Cheapside streetsweeper;
rope-makers; riding men; . Rosie the dish-seller;
Godfrey of Garlicknithe; . Griffith the Welsh;
it was teeming with tatters . by ten in the morning.
They gave Glutton good ale . to be going on with.

. . .

They were merry, morose, . and had many good drinking-songs,
and they sat there till evensong . singing in snatches,
till Glutton had gobbled . a good few gallons.
His guts started gurgling . like a grunting pigpen.

He pissed a potful . and proceeded thereafter
to blow like a bugle . out of his backside
till all who'd been awed . by his arsehole's musicianship
parried its perfume . by pinching their noses.
He couldn't stand still . or step out without his stick;
then he blundered about . like a blind busker's guide dog,
sometimes sideways . and sometimes reversing
(like the criss-cross course . of a catcher of birds
who lays lines in a maze . to enmesh his quarry).
His focus grew foggy . and failed at the doorway,
he staggered on the step . and dropped like a stone.
Clement (the cobbler) . caught him by the waist
to lift him and lay him . in his lap for a little;
but Glutton, ungrateful, . grimaced and groaned,
and puked up a pool . over the poor chap's pants –
not one cur in the county, . however clemmed,
would have guzzled that gruel . disgorged from his gullet,
so rank did it reek, . that rancid release.

Weeping and wailing, . his wife and his waif
humped him home . and helped him into bed.
His indulgence induced . great idleness in him,
so that he snored . through Saturday and Sunday;
sun waned, and he woke, . winked, wiped his eyes,
and his very first words were: . 'Where's the wassail-bowl?'
Again and again . his wife had a go at him
concerning the way . he had lived so wickedly,
until he was ashamed . and assailed by conscience,
and in crapulous remorse . he repented, praying:
'Oh God, I am Glutton, . and guilty of gourmandism –
overdoing it at dinner . and dallying over drink,
so that I've honked up . before I've gone half-a-mile,
and vomited victuals . that the poor would have valued.
I have feasted on fine fare, . even on fasting days.
I have tarried in taverns . to tope and to tittle-tattle.'
And in abject agony . he agreed to fast:
'Neither flesh nor fowl, . nor fish on a Friday,
shall sully my stomach . until such time
as Abstinence, my auntie, . allows its resumption
(though I've loathed the old hag . for as long as I've lived).'

I.M., G.E.

Chatting to dead folk isn't my line at
   all (as you well knew);
      nevertheless, I now lapse
      (just a convention, of course):

Never again will I visit the Duke's Head,
   now you've quit Putney.
      Rather, pence jingling in hand,
      I (also) head for the pier.

Callimachan

Here Philip buried the youthful Nicoteles
　　(died in his twelfth year)
　　　　of whom his father was proud,
　　　　for whom the future held hope.

Raphus cucullatus

Men call them *totersten* or *dod-aarsen;*
the whole crew made an ample meal from three,
and what remained was pickled for future use.

*

Walckvögel, being Dutch for 'disgusting bird',
men call them this; in colour they are grey;
they roam there in great plenty, insomuch
that daily the Dutch catch many and eat of them.
They capture the *Walckvögel* with their hands,
but are obliged to take good care these birds
do not attack them on the arms or legs,
their beaks being very strong and thick and hooked,
for they are wont to bite most desperate hard.

*

These *dronten, walyvogel* or *dottaerssen* –
even long boiling scarcely makes them tender,
but they remain tough, hard and leathery,
with the exception of the breast and belly,
which can be very good.

*

Five of our men
landed, provided with sticks, muskets, nets,
and sundry other necessaries for hunting.
They climbed up mountains, hills, and roamed through forests
and valleys, and in the three days they were out
they took a half a hundred *wallich-vogels*
which we then fetched on board, salted and ate.

*

There is a great bird, bigger than our swans,
with large heads, half of which is covered with skin
resembling a hood. These birds want wings,
in place of which are three or four dark quills.
The tail comprises slender, curved grey feathers.
We called them *Walgh-voghel*, for this good reason,
that the more we boiled them in gigantic vats,
the tougher and more uneatable they became.

*

This bird is more for wonder than for food,
though greasie stomaches may seek after them,
to the delicate of taste they are offensive
and of no nourishment. Men call 'em 'Doo-doo'.

En Attendant

I have been here now
for long enough to know that
you will not turn up.

Theognian [Theognis (*fl.* 530 BC)]

Futile to rail at the rasp of Privation, or
    sneer at a bankrupt –
        daily the scale dips or lifts;
        Zeus gives or else confiscates.

      *

Penury batters us, even the boldest,
    into submission,
        wrecks our resilience, hastes
        rheum and the white hair of age.

All you can do to escape is to drown or
    leap from a cliff face.
        Crushed by Privation you lose
        even the spirit to speak.

Nips

Dreams, do not invoke
my dead love or I will wake
filled with loneliness.

*

Loaves, baked fresh today,
fragrant at six this morning,
stir my sense with scents.

[Untitled]

five-lane motorway/
five-mile tailback/
Council for the Preservation
of Urban Squalor/
Keep Death on the Roads/
ten-lane motorway/
Toyota to get us
back on our feet/
Council for the Preservation
of Rural Spoliation/
Council for the Spoliation
of All You Fuckers Out There/
The Grin Belt/
The Grim Belt/
Council for the Preservation
of the Council for the Preservation/
The Black Belt/
fifteen-lane motorway/
twenty-lane/
thirty/
forty/
– what the fuck
cover the fucking lot
with a fathom of fucking asphalt
and say bollocks to it

From the Chinese

I had been in Tsai Chin' s army
for twenty-five years at war.
When I returned to my village
all was wrecked and weeds
prised through my floor, my wife
had deserted me long ago.
I drank wine and wept.

Catullan (CIII)

Do let me have back the dosh which I kindly
   lent to you last year,
      then, by all means, chatter on
      vapidly, as is your wont.

Or if you'd rather hang on to the money
   feel free to do so,
      then all I ask you is this:
      please shut your vacuous gob.

'Clear Beggars from Streets, says Blair'

(*The Times* headline 7. I. 97)

I want to clear the streets of beggars, vagrants
and people sleeping rough, and, furthermore,
clamp down on squeegee merchants loitering
at traffic lights to wash one's windscreen. Also,
I want graffiti artists put away.
I shall reclaim the streets from mendicants
and winos, addicts, people I don't like.
These 'homeless' can be downright threatening
and must be done away with – do you know,
I often drop my kids off at King's Cross
for them to take the Tube and, actually,
it's really quite a frightening place for people.
I think the basic principle is: Yes,
it's right to be intolerant of the homeless.
Do I give money to street beggars? No!
Occasionally I *do* buy *The Big Issue*,
so *that's* OK, but, really, it's appalling
that young people are sleeping in shop doorways.
So what I want is Zero Tolerance.

From the Chinese

I donate money to a beggar;
it is not much, but he has half my wealth.

I am reminded of the sage's words:
If the mendicant gets drunk tonight,
then I am happy also.

Salopian

All day, the drone of a saw,
and resin across the pines
of dark Mortimer Forest.
With each completed sever
it fell by a whining octave.

By dusk, in the clearing they'd made,
all that remained was their dust,
the dottle from someone's pipe
and ranks of seasoning limbs
weeping congealing amber.

*

The heat, the fragrance of hay,
the incontrovertible end
of summer, the country halt,
boarding the single-track train,
weeds prising the platform oblique
where they waved and waved and waved.

*

Dewed cowslips, roses, the grave
under a yew in the garden
of lichened Pipe Aston church,
a dusty Visitors' Book...

We were once there: 17th
of June 1975.

Obit

That old woman dead
in the downstairs apartment.
No more old-fangled
nether garments pegged outside
to offend our aesthetics.

[Untitled]

Inadequate lines
limited by syllables
charting lives, loves, deaths.

Tristia

Three times the river has frozen over.
Three times the black sea has frozen over.
Three years I have been here (it seems like ten)
where the solstices seem not to matter,
nights and days being the same to me (*long*);
where hostile people constantly threaten
rapine and summary execution;
where to venture out is to take great risk;
where living is flimsily established
and atrocities perpetuated;
where the smallholders are afraid to scrape
the stony dirt to achieve their pittance
(one hand ploughing, one clutching a weapon)
or tend their scruffy sheep while they listen
for the approach of hoofbeats and marching,
with nervous glances over their shoulders.

Theocritan (XXVII)

ACROTIME. Show me thy bountiful glade where thy sapling
growth is so rampant.

DAPHNIS. Come, then, and let me show thee my fast-growing
elegant cypress.

AC. Crop the grass, little goats, while I retire to
visit this neatherd.

DA. Guzzle, ye ravenous bulls, while I show this
delicate maiden
  that which she wishes to see.

*

[Now the scene changes – herewith a stand of
new-sprouted cypress.]

AC. Oh!, thou young satyr!, what art thou touching my
breasts through my blouse for?

DA. First, I desire to test these velvety
apples for ripeness.

AC. Dear God of Nature!, please do withdraw thy
hand, for I feel faint.

DA. Courage, my sweet one, why shiver so? Art thou
fearful or bashful?

AC. Why do'st thou topple me into a ditch, thus
fouling my raiment?

DA. Notice, though, how that I give thee a gentle
fur 'neath thy garment.

AC. Ah, me!, for thou hast ripped off my girdle!
Why hast thou done so?

DA. This is my Paphian offering to sub-
lime Aphrodite.

AC. Someone aproacheth!, I beg thee to stop this
which thou art doing.

DA. 'Tis but the cypress, whispering at thy
pure consummation.

AC. Oh!, thou hast torn all my underclothes off and
now I am naked!

DA. I will now give thee a covering far more
ample than they were...

[Untitled]

Bards write to the dead
'You were so this and so that' –
   corpses cannot read.
Mother and Father, *before*
you croak, I write to thank you.

OED

Two new words today,
each useless: *nimbiferous,*
also *nidifice.*

Luger

During the Second World War
my father-in-law killed a German
from whom he stole a pistol.

When we collected his stuff,
after his stroke in the 'eighties,
we gave the gun in to Old Bill.

But I should have kept it, kept it
so that I could have, now,
blown my fucking brains out.

[Untitled]

Only in abject despair they glimpse the
    solace of Word-Hoard;
        then the bright casket's lid slams.
        sealing the treasure inside.

Propertian (IV. vii)

Ghosts *do* live;
   death doesn't end all:
the pale shade cheats
   the funeral pyre.

Over my bed
   Cynthia leaned,
though her ashes lay buried
   near the noisy highway.
Sleepless with grief
   after her obsequies
I lay lamenting
   in the sheets' bleak realm.

Her hair and her eyes
   seemed the same as they were
when she was borne
   on her bier at the end;
her charred dress
   adhered to her body;
the fire had melted
   her ring of beryl;
and although the bitter
   waters of Lethe
had scorched her lips
   she spoke in a voice
charged with living breath
   as her knuckles crackled
charcoal-brittle.

   'Treacherous lover!,
faithful to nobody,
   how can you sleep
at a time like this?
   Have you forgotten
the nights we made love
   breast to breast
till we warmed the bare street
   where we coupled and coupled
under our cloaks?

Did anyone see you
prostrate with grief for me?,
    your mourning-clothes steaming
with tears of anguish?
    At least as far
as the gates, if you couldn't
    be bothered to go
any further, you could have
    asked my bearers
to walk more slowly,
    and lent the occasion
some semblance of dignity.

    And why were no fragrant
spices cast on my pyre?
    Was a bunch of cheap hyacinths
too much to ask of you?
    Could you not have breached
a bottle of wine
    and made a libation
to my spent spirit?
    But, though you deserve it,
Sextus Propertius,
    I shan't nag you now:
I know that for years
    your verses have honoured me.
May the adder hiss
    and writhe through my ribs
if I lie when I tell you
    that I have been faithful.

But now, if you're not
    besotted with Chloris,
hear what I wish:
    those poems you wrote to me,
burn them, burn them,
    make me no longer
an object of worship;
    clear from my grave
the virulent ivy
    which otherwise tangles
and twines round my bones;
    incise in stone

this noble epitaph
   that Romans may read it –
IN THE CLAY OF TIBUR
   CYNTHIA RESTS
ENDOWING GLORY
   TO ANIO'S BANKS.

And, Sextus, don't doubt
   apparitions that roam
from Elysian regions –
   such visions have weight.
By night we are free,
   unfettered shadows;
at dawn we are destined
   to turn back to Lethe
where Charon counts us
   carefully aboard.

Though others may have you now
   soon you'll be *mine*!
Together our bones
   will grind in union.'

Her indictment ended,
   I tried to embrace her,
but her shadow, like vapour,
   thinned, uncorporeal.

Distich

All that remained was to tidy the desk and
   type out the distich,
      then end the myth that they don't
      do it who *threaten* they will.